THE RUBÁIYÁT OF
OMAR KHAYYÁM

THE RUBÁIYÁT OF OMAR KHAYYÁM

Fitzgerald's interpretation,
rearranged to include new quatrains embodying
an adaptation of further thoughts
from Omar

BY

ERNEST E. LAWS

A Nadder Book
ELEMENT BOOKS LTD

© *The Estate of Ernest E. Laws* 1983
This edition first published in Great Britain 1983
by Element Books Ltd
The Old Brewery, Tisbury
Wiltshire

Text and cover design by Humphrey Stone
ISBN 0 906540 35 6

Printed by Skelton's Press
Wellingborough, Northants

Preface

Edward Fitzgerald, after the fourth version of his adaptation of some of Omar Khayyám's quatrains, wrote to Quaritch, the publisher, that his adaptations should be elaborated to present them in a new edition in which his work, as distinct from Omar Khayyám's, would be a cohesive poem. He stated that he was too weary to take that task upon himself. When he was gravely and sometimes querulously blamed, after his second edition, of having altered parts of the first edition he stated that perhaps those that would read his second version first would prefer the second. How true that can be! And how true it is that in the matter of a beautiful enough stanza or line the reader, especially the memorising reader, is loth to tolerate the slightest change of even a word, and that the very author is loth to make it! That attitude for thousands of years has been the enemy of freedom in literature, has been the unreasoning, biassed obstructor of any serious attempt to improve on the original, or the reputedly original, recorded words of anyone whomsoever including men and demi-gods and women and demi-goddesses, ancient or modern. We do not tolerate that attitude regarding other creations of man. It would be difficult to cite any material invention that was perfect at its inception. Either the inventor in person had to work on it assiduously to better, by trial and error, the result of his first conception, or others had to work on it to that effect.

[5]

I most readily admit that, in the matter of the recorded word, no one is justified in destroying any state of the originator's presentation of his conception, or to garble it in such a way as to prevent us from knowing what was exactly his conception or mental invention; nevertheless each one of us is entitled, after careful study of a conception and its presentation, by taking fresh paper to make an assiduous adaptation, having set one's spirit and talent free to do so. Likewise, at the expense of one's own means and time and by using fresh raw material without meddling with the original, one is entitled to try to adapt even a masterpiece of painting or sculpture or architecture, etc. Rubens released his genius in making adaptations of works by Titian, e.g. of his "The Fall of Man" (both paintings are in the Prado in Madrid) and of his "Garden of Love", which is in the National Gallery in Stockholm. Past persons of outstanding intellect have stated that there are no longer new ideas but only new presentations or facets or nuances of one or another of humanity's fund of ideas. Shakespeare's poems and plays could not have been made if he had not set himself utterly free to take ancient and contemporary ideas, stories and history, notions, prejudices, beliefs, tastes, customs, etc., and to give them his own brilliantly genial presentation or interpretation clothed with or in his readily acceptable fresh applications of every-day words.

It has suited certain cliques to oblige others, especially children, to accept specified texts as being ungainsayable, inspired, even sacrosanct. There is nothing sacrosanct about stanzas or quatrains attributed to Omar

[6]

Khayyám, the Persian Astronomer and Mathematician, or about the adaptation of some of them into English by Fitzgerald; and there is nothing sacrilegious about my having tried to do what Fitzgerald felt himself too weary to do. Gradually (in the long, very long course of my attempt) I not only rearranged Fitzgerald's stanzas, but also changed some of them and restored quatrains of his rejected by him; and I placed in the text any that he had put only in his preface or in his notes. I also included more than 100 quatrains of my own adaptations of some of Omar Khayyám's other thoughts, thoughts that Fitzgerald knew of but, for one reason or another, did not adapt (probably for fear of hostile contemporary opinion). Undoubtedly Omar's turn of thought is destructive of sanctimonious and social humbug.

I gravely warn all persons of weak religious sentiments and shaky faith not to read my presentation of Omar Khayyám's thoughts and my rehandling of Fitzgerald's interpretations; those of strong faith will not be shaken but rather steeled by it.

Fitzgerald did no harm to any copies of Omar Khayyám's quatrains in Persian or in any other language; they remained for anyone to use. I have not marred any text or any rendering of them, nor have I marred any Fitzgerald manuscripts or any copy of any edition of his interpretations. They all remain intact, in so far as I am concerned, and are easily available throughout the world. Any harm done, if harm can thus be done, is to myself if I have failed in the public eye in my attempt.

[7]

1   *Awake, awake! The Sun begins to rise*
    And gives to all a glimpse of Paradise.
      Forsake the arms of Sleep, and come with me
    To know the bliss that Life to sloth denies!

2   *Awake, awake, and not a sluggard lie!*
    The flower that slumbered 'neath the jewelled sky
      Is blithe in bloom and dew to greet the light;
    And owls and bats and such to shadows hie.

3   *I sometimes in my garden, flanked by friends,*
    Outstay the night, and, when the moonglow ends,
      Behold come out the living things but man
    Rejoicing while the King of Day ascends.

4   *Arise! for Morning through the dome of Night*
    Has flung the shafts that put the Stars to flight;
      And, lo! the Hunter of the East has caught
    The Sultan's turret in a noose of light.

5   *Astir! for he who drove to their dismay*
    The Moon and Stars out of the Field of Day
      And with his glance chased Night with them, has filled
    The world with his rejuvenating ray.

6   The desert Spring adorns with fragrant flowers;
     The soaring larks pour forth their song in showers;
          But you, O thriftless dreamer! are inert,
     Unmindful how you waste your precious powers.

7   Drowsing when dawn's mirage was in the sky
     I heard the Voice within the tavern cry:
          "To me! my little ones, and fill the cup
     Before the stream of life in you runs dry!"

8   And, while the cock crew, those that stood before
     The tavern shouted: "Open, then, the door!
          You know how little while we have to stay,
     And, once departed, may return no more."

9   The mystic Voice of life, resounding, says:
     "The boughs have burgeoned 'neath the morning rays;"
          And whispers warning: "Ah, make haste! for you
     Do not renew, like vines, your youthful days."

10   Ah, make the most of what we yet may spend
     Before we also into dust descend,
          Dust unto dust, forever under dust, –
     With never lute nor song nor love, nor end!

11 This is the season when the heart's desire
    Takes wing, and lovers to unite aspire,
        And gentle Zephyr is a sigh of love,
    And every star a spark from love on fire.

12 Iram indeed has gone with all its rose,
    And Jamshýd's sev'n-ring'd cup where no one knows;
        But still the ruby kindles in the vine,
    And still a garden by the water glows.

13 And David's lips are locked, but in divine
    High piping Pehleví, with "Wine, red wine!;"
        The nightingale invites the love-sick rose
    To make its pallid cheeks incarnadine.

14 Ah, countless roses summer brings, they say;
    Yes! – but where went the rose of yesterday?
        And this spring-month that wakens Earth to life
    Shall waft the sleeping dust of death away.

15 One day we sit upon the soil, and lie
    In it the next, the broken-hearted by,
        Who thought they could display their sweets yet keep
    Them from the thirsty hungry charnel fly.

16   Be wary, friend! for in this world of strife
       Our path with pitfalls to the end is rife;
           And only they that follow Nature's lead
       Shall reach in joy and peace the goal of Life.

17   Be prudent, pilgrim! for the way you wend
       Is perilous, and bolts of chance descend.
           Be mindful who you are, and whence you came,
       And whither go, and how you aim to end!

18   Whether at Naishapúr or Babylon,
       Whether the cup with sweet or bitter run,
           The wine of life keeps oozing drop by drop,
       The leaves of life keep falling, one by one.

19   So, come with me! for what have we to do
       With Kaikobád the Great or Kaikosrú?
           Nor one as strong as Zál or Rustum fear,
       Nor let a lavish Hátim hinder you!

20   And we in some oasis yet unsown
       Will seek a shelter for ourselves alone,
           Where neither slave nor tyrant ventures near.
       And peace to Mahmúd on his golden throne!

21 *We there will build for us an ample nest,*
    Secure from envy and the tiresome guest;
        And, loving each the other to the end,
    Shall be by Nature's bounty daily blest.

22 *The souls whose centre ever is the heart*
    Of Love, fear never Death's unerring dart;
        For total lovers know that love survives
    And grows should either from this life depart.

23 *Alas! though all know well that each must die*
    They hope and crave for Death to pass them by
        Ev'n in their worst decay. Ah! death comes best
    When yet the tide of love and zest runs high.

24 *To Death the lamps are like a blackened wall.*
    Dead yesterdays have gone beyond recall.
        Today is live; so live it if you can!
    To-morrow may content you or appal.

25 *Much time is lost comparing proved with new;*
    Ideals are oft the foes of good and true.
        Ah, live! Ah, live! Wait not what might be best!
    Take now the pearl of rapture offered you!

26   To me the past and future vainly call;
    And you alone can hold my heart in thrall.
       The present is my Heav'n if spent with you;
    For you, Belovéd, are my all, – my all!

27   To prove my love for you I would forgo
    Riches and health, and suffer every woe.
       Entirely I am yours; and all my care
    Is that your joy should ever greater grow.

28   Your hot enthralling glance would make all wan
    With love's desire a King of Babylon;
       And, since the placid Moon hath looked upon
    Your peerless face, her self-content is gone.

29   The Queen of Sheba would the whole world through
    Have sought a spell to make herself be you;
       King Solomon have left his wives and loves
    To be to only you forever true.

30   Your fair cool cheeks outlive the eglantine;
    Your eyes are violets, your brow divine;
       Your voice enraptures larks and nightingales;
    In port and grace a Goddess you enshrine.

31   *With rubies, pearls, and gold-emblazoned dress,*
       And musk your painted rivals court success;
          But you, disdaining every artifice,
       Have triumphed with your naked loveliness.

32   *Your mouth is richer than the nectar-flower;*
       Your hair is softer than the summer-shower;
          Your fragrance, form, and grace are Nature's pride;
       And Beauty's self is your increasing dower.

33   *Your sympathy is balm when Sorrow stings;*
       The strange caress of your long lashes brings
          Me nigh to Heav'n; your whisper thrills me while
       The nightingale her love-lorn lyric sings.

34   *A book of verse, a bough beneath the Blue,*
       A jug of wine, a loaf of bread, and you
          Beside me singing in the wilderness, –
       Oh! wilderness were Paradise anew.

35   *The longings, sighs, and moans by lovers breathed*
       The fallen angels had to us bequeathed.
          The stars are sparkling to the lilt of Love.
       In Love's glad glory Sun and Moon are wreathed.

36 Whoever deeply loves is 'neath the sway
    Of Love's compulsive moods by night and day.
        Ah! only they that love can duly prize
    The Sun's flushed face, the Moon's serene display.

37 Pretended love is like a painted flame,
    Giving nor light nor heat; and it makes game
        Of honour and romance; and mostly ends
    Its crooked course in bitterness and blame.

38 The love-pretenders wallow in the sloughs
    Of sordid ruse, and sigh their perjured vows,
        And solemnly betray because their souls
    Are steeped in lust, whose fumes to frenzy rouse.

39 With savage strength and fury faithless lust
    Defiles the innocent, and tramples trust;
        But love, which conquers vaunting lust, is true,
    Unselfish, yielding, generous and just.

40 One, then, should never let another bind
    One's heart with loathsome chains, nor cloud one's mind
        With lust in guise of love; for love is free,
    And truly sees; but slavish lust is blind.

41   The gentlest hand could make you rue its weight,
       And candid love could turn to gloomy hate.
           Clasp, therefore, friendship's hand and welcome love;
       But never let your vigilance abate!

42   "Be loved and love!" is Nature's law. Then, why,
       When Fate has willed that you be mine and I
           Be yours, should we rebel and try to thwart
       The urge that Nature bids us satisfy?

43   Although a compass at its base divides,
       It at its head in unity abides;
           So we, when parted, yet are one because
       In us true love, which sunders not, resides.

44   O Chosen of my heart, to me more dear
       Than life! why toss my soul 'twixt hope and fear?
           While you are ripe and in your prime fulfil
       My wish and make us each contented here!

45   When first your star-glance took me by surprise,
       And lit my heart, and filled me with surmise,
           My love, though I thought eyelids could debar,
       Sped straight to you from my enchanted eyes.

46   *At that grand moment all my soul's design*
      Was formed to win you, hold you ever mine
         That you and I be two in one till death.
      Oh, love me, flesh and mind, with me combine!

47   *And then my outer life and inner life, —*
      Whate'er my plight or state, in peace or strife, —
         Will be for me ecstatic joy each day
      With you as friend and loved and loving wife.

48   *Our union in our souls' orgastic kiss*
      Shall waft us far away from doubt's abyss,
         And ravish us to spheres sublime of bliss.
      Ah! only Fable boasts to better this.

49   *We are the dupes of myth when we upbraid*
      Ourselves because we love; for we were made
         For loving: all the sweets of living are
      For those that love. Be joyful, unafraid!

50   *Our souls should not be wastes of sordid woe,*
      But gardens where the blooms of gladness blow;
         So, stifle not your heart, lest thwarted love,
      In vengeance, cause your reason's overthrow!

51 *Since you nor made nor battered humankind*
Let not yourself be uselessly inclined
To shape them on your heart, as if it were
An anvil, with the hammer of your mind!

52 *With calm each sect and coterie decline,*
No matter what their vogue and vaunted sign!
Your spirit sanely free from make-believe,
And gather grapes of truth from Nature's vine!

53 *Moslems repeat their cleansing rites and pray'r*
Because from them escaped a puff of air.
The Christians must forgo the Eucharist
Because they gulped a drop or crumb aware.

54 *Ah, go, a liege of love, of wine, of song,*
With truth and honour, mirth and wit along
The ways of friendliness; and take delight
In Nature's gifts; and have no foe but wrong!

55 *A garden be your realm, wherein there are*
Choice flowering plants and birds from near and far;
And, when the blooms and songsters all depart,
Imagine that they go to greet a star!

56   Good friend, the rod of strength, the sheath of joy
      Are precious treasures that we should employ.
          All self-frustration, self-inflicted pain
      Are worthless dross in souls of base alloy.

57   The mystics claim that sorrow is divine;
      But I will not for any cause repine;
          For I am sure that in ourselves there is
      For every ill the secret anodyne.

58   Adam and Eve! how poignant must have been
      Your first embraces in the Garden scene!
          A vengeful feast was that forbidden fruit:
      Why else are we constrained such griefs to glean?

59   The nightingale in sadness crooned this strain:
      "An hour of bliss may breed a life of pain."
          A screen of tears hides Heav'n from me. Hell's flames
      Are but the sparks from fires that eat my brain.

60   Yet, though Good Fortune may precede a fall,
      Why spurn her when on you she deigns to call?
          A special boon is such a grace, ev'n if
      It leave an aftertaste far worse than gall.

61   *Pursue your path with Pleasure hand-in-hand*
      The while your steps approach the doubtful land!
         I dream that friends now dead all laugh and sing:
      Perhaps at last they live and understand.

62   *It would be folly, freely choosing pain,*
      To throw away the present joy to gain –
         What future for ourselves? who knows not if,
      Although now breathing, we may breathe again.

63   *Some for the glories of this world, and some*
      Sigh for the Prophet's Paradise to come.
         Ah, take the cash and let the credit go,
      Nor heed the rumble of a distant drum!

64   *Hark to the blowing rose about us! "Lo!*
      Laughing" she says "into the world I blow;
         Enjoy my beauty, take me if you will,
      Or let my riches with the breezes go!"

65   *If in the Prophet's Paradise may stand*
      Only the wine-and-love-abjuring band,
         That promised Realm of Happiness must be
      As gloomy as a gaunt and sunless land.

66   Because they say that after death the prize
      Is wine and song and love that satisfies,
          Accept such blessings gladly while on Earth,
      And thus prepare yourself for Paradise!

67   The worldly hope men set their hearts upon
      Turns ashes; or it prospers; and anon,
          Like snow upon the desert's dusty face,
      Lighting a little hour or two, is gone.

68   And those that husbanded the golden grain,
      And those that flung it to the wind like rain,
          To no such precious treasure ever turn
      As, buried once, men want dug up again.

69   All futile hopes, regrets, and gnawing care
      Deprive today of peace, and breed despair;
          And they that flinch for fear a blow be struck
      Allure it, and are stricken unaware.

70   Ah, my Belověd, fill the cup that clears
      To-day of vain remorse and phantom fears!
          To-morrow? Why! to-morrow I myself
      May be with yesterday's forgotten years.

71   Think, in this battered caravanserai,
      Whose portals are alternate night and day,
          How Sultan after Sultan with his pomp
      Abode his destined hour and went his way!

72   On seeing ruins where, before, in view
      Were fanes whose towers soared the heavens to,
          I asked a pilgrim: "There ruled who?" And, lo!
      A widowed ring-dove echoed me: "Who, who?"

73   They say the lion and the lizard keep
      The courts where Jamshýd gloried and drank deep;
          And over that great hunter Bahrám's head
      The wild ass stamps, but cannot break his sleep.

74   I sometimes think that never blows so red
      The rose as where heroic lovers bled;
          That every hyacinth the garden wears
      Has sprung from where once lay a loved one's head;

75   And that its velvet robe the tulip dyes
      In tears that fell from Love's imploring eyes;
          That drowsy poppies sip the drug of dreams
      From dew distilled of lovers' vows and sighs.

76   And this reviving herb, whose tender green
       Graces the river-lip on which we lean, –
          Ah, lean upon it lightly! for who knows
       From what once luscious lip it springs unseen.

77   Lo! some we loved, the loveliest and the best
       That from his vintage rolling Time hath prest,
          Have drunk their cup a round or two before
       And one by one crept silently to rest.

78   And we that now make merry in the room
       They left, which summer dresses in new bloom,
          Must underneath the couch of earth descend, –
       Ourselves to be, perhaps, a couch. For whom?

79   With fervour live your fleeting span of light;
       For soon enough shall come eternal night;
          And then your soul shall go, beyond recall, –
       And who knows whither? – on her final flight.

80   We are the devotees of love and wine,
       Our mystic eyes from eager faces shine,
          Our hearts beat strong with life, our minds are free
       Because our souls are steeped in truth divine.

81   Alike to those that for to-day take care
And those that after some to-morrow stare
      Muezzins from the Tower of Darkness cry:
"Fools, your reward is neither here nor there!"

82   And they that burn in heart for who may burn
In hell, whose fire themselves may feed in turn,
      Why do they wail: "O Allah, pity them!"?
Why! – who are they to teach, and He to learn?

83   Yes! why as dismal as a doomsday knell
Do bigots take upon themselves to quell
      Our song, insult our guests, upset our Wine
And claim they buttress Virtue's citadel?

84   For they, who thus condemn our merriment
And claim that we because of it are sent
      To hell, are spawn of sin and have no call
To judge in Allah's name our day's content.

85   The wanton barters publicly the bowl
Of lust for sage or fool to drug the soul.
      The prudes, who fain would wither her with scorn,
Oft play behind the scenes the wanton's role.

86   *We puny human creatures are a blend*
     Of water, earth, and air, and fire; and tend,
        As being each both wolf and lamb, to prey
     Upon ourselves, and one another rend.

87   *The few are leaders, most are too obscure;*
     The few are champions, most are too demure;
        The few are sacred, most are too profane;
     But all of us have feelings called impure.

88   *Are myths that prophets say are facts divine*
     Better than dreams in sleep or dreams in Wine?
        Must we give heed to scowling hypocrites,
     Who feign that life's delights are swill for swine?

89   *It seems that in each place for prating prayer*
     Is fostered futile hope or dread despair;
        But phantom fears do not assault the soul
     That knows eternal Love is everywhere.

90   *A lifetime I have sinned; and surely know*
     That Love forgives me still as long ago.
        Another lifetime I would sin to prove
     That Love will ever full forgiveness show.

91   O threats of hell and hopes of Paradise!
      One thing is certain in this life of lies,
          One thing, – the rest is mainly mere surmise –:
      The flower that once has blown forever dies.

92   Await for Paradise till I am dead?
      Nay! here I can, whene'er by Fancy led,
          Beneath the Sedrah by the Kóuser mate
      With fluxless houris, nor be surfeited.

93   A valley with a river running through,
      And wild flowers dancing, drunk with honey-dew,
          And larks aloft and lithe gazelles at play, –
      Oh! that were more than Eden if with you.

94   The birds outpour impassioned rhapsodies;
      The mating blooms inebriate the breeze;
          Clouds spread their cooling sails. Ah, live with zest!
      For brief are shade and scent and harmonies.

95   The thought of after-death disturbs not those
      That would enjoy the gifts this life bestows.
          Come touch the lute, and sing, and love, and leave
      The dead to rise, or in the dust repose!

96   *The revelations of the saint and seer*
    And wizard, who lay claim to light our sphere,
       Are fables all that they, aroused from sleep,
    Recount, and then forever disappear.

97   *Strange, is it not? that, of the countless throng*
    That through the Door of Darkness passed along
       Not one returns to tell us where they went,
    Or whether any way is right or wrong?

98   *Time watches in each era passing by*
    Impostors give the law, and prophesy,
       And warring fiends make man's trim world a waste,
    And saviours as forsaken losers die.

99   *And still the motley caravan jogs past;*
    The few are feasting while the many fast;
       To-morrow's slave, who yesterday was free,
    To-day is in the role of tyrant cast.

100   *Virtue is trodden down, and vice enthroned;*
    Courage is chained, and cowardice condoned;
       And what, before, by most was counted wise
    Is now by most as foolishness disowned.

101   *Yet Truth survives, and only Truth can give*
        The law of right, and set us free to live
           In love and peace; and so I wryly smile
        When falsehood masks in Truth's prerogative.

102   *The lie that some mistake for truth appears*
        Quite plain to those that know the hidden spheres;
           In quest of Wisdom, then, 'tis best for us
        To seal our lips and hearken to the seers.

103   *The fosterers of falsehood dread the flash*
        Of Truth; it yet could be unwise and rash
           To proffer undiluted truth; for they
        That feed on lies treat simple fact as trash.

104   *Since countless years ago a cryptic tribe,*
        Who scorn the law and live on lie and bribe,
           Have roamed the world, and duped and biassed us.
        Why bear we them and to their frauds subscribe?

105   *Why! famous saints and sages, who discussed*
        Commandingly the rights and wrongs, are thrust
           Like broken idols down; their lore is scorned,
        Their code disowned; their mouths are stopped with dust.

106 Ah! eagerly when young I, too, had bent
    Mine ear to subtle specious argument
        In halls of saint and sage; and yet came out
    No more enlightened than when in I went.

107 With them the seed of wisdom did I sow,
    And night and day I toiled to make it grow;
        And this was all the harvest that I reaped:
    "I came like water, and like wind I go."

108 I used to think that I was sage and rare;
    Yet I in any field was but a tare,
        A droplet shaped in common pots, a grain
    Of salt in seas, a puff of smoke in air.

109 To spheres unseen I sent my soul to spell
    Some letter of that After-Life; and, – well!
        My soul came back, and said that all she learned
    Is that within herself is heav'n and hell.

110 Heav'n is fruition of the soul's desire,
    And hell is woe that sets the soul on fire,
        And shows the darkness out of which she came
    And into which she shall so soon expire.

111   *Up from Earth's centre through the seventh gate*
    I rose, and on the throne of Saturn sate,
        And many knots unravelled by the road;
    But ne'er the master-knot of human fate.

112   *There was the door to which I found no key;*
    There was the veil through which I might not see;
        And Voices talked of us and Him; but none
    Unlocked the door or raised the veil for me.

113   *Land could not answer nor the seas that mourn*
    In flowing purple of their Lord forlorn,
        Nor boundless space with all its signs revealed,
    Or in the cloak of sombre clouds withdrawn.

114   *Not earth, nor air, nor water gave the clue*
    To teach the soul to know the false and true;
        But Heav'n's revealing fire would blaze, methought,
    And end the night that covers me, – and you.

115   *Therefore with faith to awful Heav'n I cried,*
    Asking: "What lamp has Destiny to guide
        Her little children stumbling in the dark?"
    "Only a sightless instinct." Heav'n replied.

116   Then to the Force in me that works behind
The veil of sense I turned my groping mind,
     And heard these solemn words: "You never here
Will know the truth; so, be to me resigned!"

117   And last I leaned to this poor earthen urn
The secret meaning of my life to learn;
     And lip to lip it whispered: "While you live
Drink! for, once dead, you never shall return."

118   Poor urn, which spoke those accents fugitive! —
I think that formerly it too did live
     And drink; and that its passive mouth I kiss
Did countless burning kisses take and give;

119   For, in the market-place, one fasting-day,
I watched the potter thumping his wet clay;
     And with its all obliterated tongue
It murmured: "Gently, brother, gently, pray!,

120   "Myself was once like you, and, till I died,
Was steering mid the rocks of greed and pride.
     The handles that you mould upon me were
My hands that fondled once my loving bride."

121   *And later, when with the departing day*
       Slunk hunger-stricken Rámazán away,
          I sat alone within the potter's house
       Surrounded by the serried shapes of clay, –

122   *Shapes of all sorts and uses, great and small,*
       For Sultan, for his harem, for the thrall, –
          Mute shapes all resting, happy that no more
       Were hagglers there to maul and bid and brawl.

123   *And once again among them there was heard*
       A whisper, – as it were a force was stirred
          By tongues not yet by death forever stilled –,
       Which mine ear kindled into living word.

124   *And one was saying: "Was it near in vain*
       My substance, which in common earth had lain,
          Was deftly shaped? for soon it will be smashed
       And trampled into common earth again."

125   *Another said: "Not ev'n a peevish boy*
       Would break the bowl from which he drank in joy.
          And He, who made the vessel lovingly
       Will He His work in after-wrath destroy?"

126   *None answered this; but, after silence, spake*
        A lowly vessel of ungainly make:
           "They swear at me for leaning all awry.
        What! did the hand, then, of the Potter shake?"

127   *"Why!" said another, "some there are that tell*
        Of One that threatens He will toss to hell
           The luckless pots He marred in making. Pah!
        He is the Merciful; and all is well."

128   *And then to each of that loquacious lot*
        There cried a sufi pipkin, – waxing hot –:
           "All this of pot and potter!, – tell me, then,
        Who is the potter, pray, and who the pot?"

129   *"Well!" answered one, "a potter once was I,*
        And now my clay with long neglect is dry;
           But fill me with the old familiar juice,
        Methinks I might recover by and by!"

130   *And, while the vessels one by one were speaking,*
        In looked the new-born Moon that all were seeking;
           So each one jogged another: "Brother, brother,
        Now for the porter's shoulder-knot a-creaking!"

131   *The porter, then, as from the bulging skin*
        The wine was gurgling, cried above the din:
           "Why nods the needy worshipper outside
        While Pleasure's Temple is prepared within?"

132   *And hath not such a story from of old*
        Down man's successive generations rolled
           Of clay, like that from which those murmurs came,
        Cast by the Maker into human mould?

133   *So, when at Rámazán in cellars deep*
        The wine lies hid, and love must secret keep
           The tryst, and some, to foil fanatic hate,
        Frequent the mosque (and in its shadow sleep),

134   *Be of good cheer! – the sullen month will die,*
        The old Moon fainting falter from the sky,
           All meagre, bent, and wan with gloom and fast,
        And soon a new Moon gladden every eye.

135   *Come, fill the cup, and in the fire of Spring*
        The winter-garment of repentance fling!
           The Bird of Time has but a little way
        To fly; and, lo!, the Bird is on the wing.

136   *Indeed the idols I have loved so long*
Have done my credit in this world much wrong, –
    Have drowned my glory in a shallow cup,
And sold my reputation for a song.

137   *When once a brutal wind my wine had spilled*
I said: "O Allah! You my bliss have killed;
    For You lurched in and overturned my cup.
'Tis You, perhaps, are drunk and evil-willed."

138   *And, as it seemed He gave my face a smack,*
I said: "Some mortals master wrath's attack.
    And You! who punish me for hasty words, –
Have You a failing that some mortals lack?"

139   *But I was drunk and bold; yet soon was sad.*
Would I were never staidly sane or mad,
    And ne'er outstripped, or lagged behind, the Age,
And ne'er were over-good or over-bad!

140   *Still, though the cup has played the Infidel*
And robbed me of my Robe of Honour, well! –
    I wonder often what the vintners buy
One half so precious as the wine they sell.

141   Oh! I repent my churlish self-display
       When I misuse that liquid gem, and bay
           The Moon with ribaldry and witless din,
       And spoil with vain regret the after-day.

142   Indeed I vowed repentance oft before; —
       And was I ever sober when I swore? —
           But Youth and Spring, who came with roses decked,
       My threadbare penitence to pieces tore.

143   Alas! that spring should vanish with the rose,
       That youth's sweet-scented manuscript should close!
           The nightingale that in the branches sang,
       Ah! — whence and whither flown again, who knows?

144   Would but the fountain of the desert yield
       One glimpse, if dimly yet indeed revealed,
           To which the fainting traveller might spring
       As springs the trampled herbage of the field!

145   A moment's halt, a momentary taste
       Of Being from the Well amid the Waste!
           The Sun is setting. Lo! the caravan
       Draws near the Night of Nothing. O make haste, —

146   *Make haste to live in full the little time*
        That Fate allots you ere you pass your prime,
          Or Earth, from whom you issued, take you back
        And breed some other creatures in your slime!

147   *Quick, quick! In waiting I am older now;*
        And Day goads on my heart and thoughts; his brow
          Will lour and darken when his eyelid, Night,
        Droops down. This bubble life all tints endow;

148   *But, like the full-blown rose by winds laid bare,*
        The bubble at a shock returns to air.
          The Sun hath seen such bubbles burst as would,
        If we but dreamed them, madden with despair.

149   *Ah, fill the cup! What boots it to repeat*
        How time is slipping underneath our feet?
          Doubtful to-morrow, bungled yesterday, –
        Why fret for them if your to-day be sweet?

150   *Like tulips, then, which for their morning sup*
        Of heav'nly vintage from the soil look up,
          Lift up your head and look for Life till Heav'n
        To Earth invert you, – like an empty cup!

151   And fear not lest Existence, closing your
        Account and mine should see the like no more!
            Eternal Sáki from the bowl has poured
        By billions drops like us, and yet shall pour.

152   When you and I behind the Veil are past, –
        Oh, what a long long while the World shall last!
            The World our coming and departure heeds
        No more than Ocean heeds a pebble-cast.

153   The dead rest? Let them rest! The living are
        Too often weights that stop our rising far.
            Do not depend on any mortal thing
        If you would travel with the Guiding-Star!

154   The Guiding-Star is Truth, – impartial, right,
        Compassionate and sure; and they that plight
            Themselves to Truth shall know Eternal Light;
        But falsehood's friends are lost in lightless night.

155   Although against you all the world might rage
        And death confront you, spurn dishonour's wage,
            And never deal with those that seek your doom,
        And rather starve than cringe in any cage!

156   *It is a sorry lack of finer sense*
        To place in others boundless confidence:
           To count too much on them would undermine
        The strength you need to be your own defence.

157   *Forget you were forgotten yesterday,*
        Nor wait upon to-morrow's yea or nay,
           Be loth to voice your bliss or anguish lest
        The latter swell, the former shrink away!

158   *Not even to a shade should you disclose*
        The secret no one else but Allah knows.
           And only with the true be intimate;
        For friendship in the false is but a pose.

159   *Alas! the human rulers of the Earth*
        Have seldom more to vaunt than might or birth;
           And, fed on flatt'ry served by sycophants,
        Are prone to flout the truth and stifle worth.

160   *A Prince unjust is seed that breeds disdain;*
        A vicious Prince a weed that spoils good grain;
           A wilful Prince a steed the curb must tame;
        A witless Prince a reed that breaks with strain.

161 *A Chief or King or Queen or President*
  That o'er the world could wield sole government,
   As if divine, would yet be at the beck
  Of his or her unruly clownish vent.

162 *The despots boast because they herd their slaves*
  And through their labour cram their treasure-caves.
   The just rejoice to guide a free man's will
  By love, and give what everybody craves.

163 *The Victors that in greed on others trod*
  May be forsaken by their Battle-God.
   They should not flaunt their might; for on their backs
  The erstwhile serfs will ply revenge's rod.

164 *Unwise are they that light the fires of hate*
  For words and whims, and then repent too late.
   And though they tell you that revenge is sweet,
  Befriend your foe and Peace will grace your state.

165 *Ah, gently let the needy take a seat*
  To share with you your store of wine and wheat!
   And you will thus, in giving others joy,
  Nobly your own increase and make more sweet.

166 *In you is neither fear nor cringing bent;*
  And yet I counsel you: "Till life be spent
   So act to all your guests as if you are
  Their slave; and dread to cause them discontent!"

167 *If ever callously you send despair*
  To pierce a trusting heart that knew no care,
   Rest not until you cure the ill, and bring
  Delight to dwell where sorrow made its lair!

168 *Because its purse is filled with gold the rose*
  Uplifts its head; in want dejected grows
   The violet. Ah! even Beauty wilts
  Unless for her the Fount of Fortune flows.

169 *Yet they that have sufficient for to-day*
  And bartered not their souls or pride to pay
   For it, though counted poor, are rich because
  Their peace depends on no one's yea or nay.

170 *And they that crush their grapes and grind their corn*
  On land they own, and there from morn to morn,
   Enslaving no one, live secure and free
  Are on the breast of Fortune fondly borne.

171   Contented is the heart that pays no heed
      To hate, and lives for Truth, devoid of greed,
          And thus is free from shameful servitude
      To any man or any man-made creed.

172   Perplext no more with human or divine,
      To-morrow's tangle I to Fate resign,
          And lose my fingers in your tresses, – O
      My cypress-slender minister of wine!

173   And, – if the wines we drink, the lips we press
      Begin and end, like all, in nothingness, –
          Know, then, we ever are as heretofore
      We were: hereafter we shall not be less!

174   So, – when the Angel by the river-brink
      Finds us at last, and, offering the Drink
          Of Darkness, summons to our lips our soul
      To quaff it, – we shall not in terror shrink.

175   Why! if the soul by casting dust aside
      Can freely on the air of Heaven ride,
          Would it not be a crime for her so long
      In this clay carcase crippled to abide?

176   'Tis but a tent where takes his one day's rest
       A Sultan to the Realm of Death addrest;
          The Sultan rises, and the mute ferrásh
       Strikes, and prepares, it for another guest.

177   Would you that bubble of Existence spend
       About the secret? Quick about it Friend!
          A hair, perhaps, divideth false from true;
       Nor can we tell on what our lots depend, –

178   A hair, perhaps, divideth false from true,
       Yea! – and a single cipher were the clue,
          Could we but find it, to the Treasure-House,
       And, peradventure, to the Master too,

179   Whose secret presence through Creation's veins
       Slipping quicksilver-like eludes our pains
          And takes all shapes, from Máh to Máhi; yet
       They change and perish all; but He remains, –

180   A moment guessed, then fades behind the Fold
       Of Darkness that is round the drama roll'd,
          Which for the pastime of Eternity
       He doth Himself contrive, enact, behold;

181   For, – let professor, preacher, doctor screech
       Of what they will and what they will not! – each,
          When called, must play the part by Him assigned,
       And all must learn what only He can teach.

182   And that inverted bowl we call the sky,
       Whereunder crawling cooped we live and die,
          Lift not your hands to it for help; for it
       As impotently moves as you or I.

183   And, if in vain down on the stubborn floor
       Of Earth and up to Heaven's fast-shut door
          You gaze to-day while you are you, how, then,
       To-morrow when you shall be you no more?

184   How long, how long, in stupid, vain pursuit
       Of this and that endeavour and dispute?
          Better be merry with the friendly grape
       Than sadden after none, or bitter fruit.

185   For I, who spent my day and night to sew
       The tent of Wisdom, burned in fires of woe,
          And Truth stripped off the veil of make-believe,
       And Nature's broker priced my learning low.

186   *My heart said: "Head! what have you taught me, yet?"*
My head said: "A begins the alphabet."
    My heart replied: "You also said that one
Begins the sum to which no end is set."

187   *They call me coward when I serve the throne,*
And traitor when I wend my way alone.
    Ah! ev'n were one a saint it would be well,
It seems, to hide one's light, and be unknown.

188   *The more I lived I better understood*
That ever what is natural is good;
    For sect and caste and make-believe befoul
The stream of universal humanhood.

189   *Whilst to and fro in doubt I swung aghast*
Life's bounties wildly to the winds I cast,
    And ne'er enjoyed one hour of full content.
Ah, would that mortals could repair the past!

190   *And so all doctrines gladly I forgot;*
And peace came only when I cut the knot
    Of doubt and knew that all our theories
Can neither recreate nor change our lot.

191   Therefore, my friend, I made with brave carouse
       A fertile second marriage in my house, —
           Divorced old barren Reason from my bed,
       And took the daughter of the vine to spouse.

192   For, though "Is not" and "Is" with rule and line,
       And "Up-and-down" by logic I define,
           Of all that one should care to fathom I
       Was never deep in anything but wine.

193   Ha! but my computations, people say,
       Reduced the World to better reck'ning? — Nay!
           'Twas only striking from the calendar
       Unborn To-morrow, buried Yesterday.

194   I tell you this: when, started from the goal,
       Over the flaming back of heaven's foal
           The Pleiades and Jupiter they flung,
       In my predestined plot of dust and soul

195   The Vine had struck a fibre, which about
       If clings my being, let the bigot flout!
           Of my base metal may be filed a key
       That shall unlock the door he howls without.

196   And this I know: whether the one True Light
      Kindle to love or wrath-consume me quite,
         One flash of it within the tavern caught, –
      Better than in the temple lost outright;

197   For lately by the tavern door agape
      Came shining through the dusk an angel-shape
         That on the shoulder bore an amphora
      And bid me taste. And lo! it was the Grape, –

198   The Grape that can with logic absolute
      The two-and-seventy jarring sects confute, –
         The Sovereign Alchemist that in a trice
      Can life's base metal into gold transmute, –

199   The Mighty Mahmúd, Overwhelming Lord,
      Who all the misbelieving louring horde
         Of fears and sorrows that infest the soul
      Scatters before Him with his whirlwind sword.

200   Must I, then, spurn that nectar in disgust,
      Scared by some after-reck'ning, given trust,
         Or lured by hope of some diviner drink
      When life's frail cup is crumbled into dust?

201 *Why, – if the Grape is Allah's Gift, who dare*
Blaspheme the teeming cluster as a snare?
  A Blessing, we should use it, should we not?
And if a curse, why, then, who set it there?

202 *For us He baits a trap at every turn;*
Our lusts, if we resist, will deeper burn.
  Does He command us shun the odour, sight,
Sound, taste and touch for which He makes us yearn?

203 *If He has made our senses, and enchains*
Our thoughts to love, and heats and swells our veins,
  And bids us sow and grow the seed, – can He
Damn us if we react as He ordains?

204 *Can He with crafty pitfall, hidden gin,*
Beset the way we are to wander in, –
  Can He predestine us to evil so –,
And justly still impute our fall to sin?

205 *Ah! "He is bountiful and gives", they say,*
"The strength we need to bear our load each day."
  Yet, who but slaves would cringe to One that had
Coerced our race to live that wretched way?

206   *So, leave the wits to wrangle and discuss,*
        And solve these problems, if they can! And thus,
           We, in our corner of the hubbub, shall
        Make game of what is making game of us.

207   *The wheel that dauntless Destiny has twirled*
        Across the crust of this bewild'ring world
           Reveals our role and cue; and we, on time,
        Into the tears and ribaldry are hurled.

208   *We are no other than a moving row*
        Of magic shadow-shapes that come and go
           Round with the Sun-illumined lantern held
        In midnight by the Master of the show;

209   *But helpless pieces of the game He plays*
        Upon this chequer-board of nights and days,
           Hither and thither moves and mates and slays,
        And each one in the crypt of Nothing lays.

210   *The ball no question makes of where it goes,*
        But blindly speeds with any player's blows;
           And He, who tossed us down upon the field,
        He knows about it all, – He knows, – He knows.

211   The Moving Finger writes, and, having writ,
      Moves on; nor sultan, prophet, saint nor wit
          Can lure it back to cancel any word,
      Nor streams of tears wash out a stroke of it.

212   With Earth's first Clay He did the last man's knead,
      In it of ev'ry harvest sowed the seed.
          Yea! the first Morning of Creation wrote
      The reck'ning that the Final Dawn shall read.

213   Yesterday this day's madness did prepare,
      To-morrow's triumph, silence or despair.
          Drink, for we know not whence we came nor why,
      Drink, for we know not why we go nor where!

214   Into this Universe, and why not knowing
      Nor whence, like water willy-nilly flowing;
          And out of it, like wind along the waste,
      We know not whither, willy-nilly blowing.

215   What! we, unasked, are hurried hither! — whence?
      And, still unasked are hurried whither hence?
          Ah, drown injustice in the cup, nor praise
      This wretched state of human impotence!

216   *Nay, I for dread of some malignant face*
       Will not eat dirt and call injustice Grace:
          There's no true Seeker but would bar to me
       His fellowship, were I to prove so base.

217   *What! He from senseless nothing can provoke*
       A conscious something to resent the yoke
          Of unpermitted pleasure under pain
       Of everlasting penalties if broke!

218   *What! — from the hapless creature be repaid*
       Pure gold for what was lent him dross-allayed;
          Sue for a debt he never did contract
       And cannot answer! O the knavish trade!

219   *Let Allah, then, — if He of clay could make*
       Our kind, and set in Paradise the Snake, —
          For all the sin that stains the human face
       Requite our griefs and our forgiveness take!

220   *If I myself upon a careless creed*
       Have loosely strung the jewel of good deed,
          Let this at least be credited to me:
       That one for two I never did misread!

221   *Like other myst'ries in our boundless space,*
       Infinity is one I do not face:
          They bruise the soul and mar the ease of man:
       I joy in work with which my wits keep pace.

222   *O help me, friend, to foil rebuffs of Chance,*
       Until the end with love my life enhance,
          Forgive my faults, remember how we soared
       To peaks of light in our ecstatic trance!

223   *I tried to see behind the Veil again,*
       And heard the Voice intoning this refrain:
          "If you are neither loved nor are in love
       You counter Nature's course, and live in vain."

224   *Ah, when the Sun's hot sighs tight buds unclose,*
       And larks sing long, and bees be-tongue the rose,
          'Tis only he and she deserve to breathe
       That rise impassioned after Love's repose.

225   *If ever you, Belovéd, were to fly*
       So far that I to you could ne'er be nigh,
          I too, like stricken birds that pine alone,
       Would flutter into solitude to die.

226   *How total was our loving from the start,*
    Although we sometimes grieved each other's heart.
        Our harmony was not complete; and, yet,
    We found scant Peace if we remained apart.

227   *In vain, while Love the passions would express,*
    I strove to break the spell of their caress.
        Alas! to no one dared I plead my plight.
    What bitter happiness! What sweet distress!

228   *It seems that spiteful Envy sprouts a thorn*
    To mar the bliss of any creature born.
        Alas! whenever Fortune favoured me,
    Chagrin soon loomed to make my soul forlorn.

229   *If babes unborn could know what grief and gloom*
    We each endure in Earth's forbidding room, –
        Could they but hear the tales that we can tell, –
    They would desire to end within the womb.

230   *"Let's quit the quest for Wisdom's Golden Fleece,"*
    Some say, "and then our miseries will cease,
        And Fortune smile." Perhaps; for shameless frauds
    And dolts so often prosper here in peace.

231   Would but some wingéd Angel, ere too late,
      Delay the yet unfolded scroll of Fate,
          And make the stern Recorder otherwise
      Enregister, or quite obliterate!

232   Allah outdid Himself creating fear
      And grief. And roll by roll His winds shall veer
          The scrolls of Fate; and souls shall stain each roll
      With tears, – in dread of what awaits them here.

233   'Twere better far to cancel from the scroll
      Of Universe each luckless human soul,
          Than drop by drop to feed the flood that grows
      Hoarser with anguish as the ages roll.

234   Has Hell by anyone been visited?
      Let them reply that are on fancies fed!
          And I shall calmly go my simple way,
      Not others mock, but give to them their head.

235   My Love! could you and I with Fate conspire
      To grasp this sorry scheme of things entire,
          Would not we shatter it to bits, and then
      Remould it nearer to the Heart's Desire?

236   The Heart desires that want and warfare end,
       That Wisdom guide, and place on worth depend,
          That Love be Ruler, Beauty's youth endure,
       And humankind be ev'ry creature's friend.

237   Ah, You, who are my Light and never wane!
       Yon waxing Moon that finds us once again
          Will rise and look for You and me some night
       Through this same garden, but — for me in vain!

238   So, — when, my Loved One, You, like her, shall pass
       Among the guests star-scattered on the grass, —
          Pause with the Wine of Joy where I was wont
       To be, and there spill out a brimming glass!

239   There's not a drop that from our cups we throw
       For earth to drink of, but may steal below
          To quench the fire of anguish in some eye
       There hidden — far beneath, and long ago.

240   Ah, with the Grape my fading life supply,
       And with the Grape embalm me when I die,
          And wrap me in a shroud of vine-leaf; then
       In some frequented garden let me lie!

241   *Where ev'n my buried body such a snare*
        Of vintage shall fling up into the air
           As not a Saint or Seeker passing by
        But shall be overtaken unaware.

242   *And there resorting from the midday heat*
        Surviving friends shall one another greet,
           And rest upon the green beneath the boughs
        Whose leaves and petals cushion my retreat.

243   *And they, whose inner life gives them release*
        Because its truth can neither change nor cease,
           Will deeply think beside me there, and know,
        I trust, a full, enduring sense of peace.

244   *Ah! when at last I mingle into clay,*
        Knead it with wine, and mould a cup, and say:
           Once this was Omar, Bard of Love and Truth.
        He lived with zest, and died without dismay.

Glossary

Bahrám : a Persian King and hunter.

Hátim : a pre-Moslem chieftain of proverbial, generous hospitality.

Iram : a fabulous garden, now sunk somewhere in the sands of Arabia.

Jamshýd : a legendary Persian King, (founder of Persepolis), possessor of a divining cup inscribed with seven heavens, seven planets, seven seas etc., symbolishing the Universe; he was the Sun-King and, holding his cup, he held the world.

Kaikobád : a mythical Persian King.

Kaikosrú : a mythical Persian King.

Kóuser : the headstream of the Moslem Paradise.

Máh to Máhi : Moon to Fish; the Earth is supposed to rest on Pisces.

Mahmud : a powerful Sultan, who ruled in Afghanistan and parts of NW India.

Naishápúr : the city where Omar was born.

Pehleví : the old Heroic language of Persia before the Arab conquest.

Rustum : *Zál's son, "Hercules" of Persia.*

Sákí : cupbearer.

Saturn : Lord of the seventh heaven.

Sedrah : the lotus tree in the Moslem Paradise.

Zál : born with white hair and reared by a bird, was strong.